NEW HORIZON[S]

In

Life, Art & Poetry

Imagination and Innovation A Personal Perspective

DR. WILLIAM CLARK

AuthorHouse™ UK
1663 Liberty Drive
Bloomington, IN 47403 USA
www.authorhouse.co.uk
UK TFN: 0800 0148641 (Toll Free inside the UK)
UK Local: 02036 956322 (+44 20 3695 6322 from outside the UK)

Because of the dynamic nature of the Internet, any web addresses or links contained in this book may have changed since publication and may no longer be valid. The views expressed in this work are solely those of the author and do not necessarily reflect the views of the publisher, and the publisher hereby disclaims any responsibility for them.

Any people depicted in stock imagery provided by Getty Images are models, and such images are being used for illustrative purposes only.
Certain stock imagery © Getty Images.

This book is printed on acid-free paper.

ISBN: 978-1-7283-5526-9 (sc)
ISBN: 978-1-7283-5525-2 (e)

Print information available on the last page.

Published by AuthorHouse 09/18/2020

authorHOUSE

New Horizons

Dr. William Clark

**Imagination and Innovation
A Personal Perspective
In Life, Art & Poetry**

Contents :

Dr Clark is the first recipeint of an award of distinction for
an outstanding contribution to the specialty of orthodontics.

Dr Clark is recognised worldwide as a teacher and innovator
in orthodontics. He founded the first full time orthodontic practice
in Scotland in 1965 and went on to develop major innovations in
orthodontics and functional therapy to improve patients appearance
and prospects in life.

Read the companion volume 'Faces & Braces' for an account of
his innovations in orthodontics to Treat Yourself to a Brilliant Smile.

However this book is not based on his professional career but
illustrates a personal perspective and keen interest in art, poetry
and a philoosophy of life that is relevant to the human condition
and contemporary society.

A Personal Perspective

Let me first explain the basis for this book. I am not an artist and have no formal training in art. My experience in art dates back to the1980's when I followed the first part of a correspondence course on drawing and painting by the Paris ABC School of Art. This was based on four volumes principally concerned with representing the visible world or "Imitating Nature".
The intention was to treat drawing and colouring together, since the two skills are inseparably linked.

Art is about creation and creation is primarily a personal adventure. The course consisted of topics, themes and activities, leaving complete freedom of interpretation and expression. There were no restrictions or set formulas, but merely hints and guidelines to enable the participant to search and discover and to express a personal experience in art.

Each chapter included a series of activites and assignments to train the hand and the eye. Unfortunately activities were home based with no need to travel to Paris! Positive feedback was offered by completing each assignment and submitting the work for review by a professional artist.

I enjoyed the course immensely but only managed to complete the first six chapters of the first volume before Planet Orthodontics occupied my time and did not enable me to complete the course. I rediscovered my earlier work at the tender age of 83 and was inspired to revisit my artistic experience of the 1980's. I hope you enjoy my combination of Art & Poetry.

Floral Art

New Horizons

Candlestick

This book is an expresssion of the author's appreciation and passion for the arts, including personal experience in drawing, painting, poetry and prose with observations on the human condition in contemporary society.

Home & Hearth

This chapter is a personal introduction to our home in the county of Fife and the surrounding countryside on the east coast of Scotland. We live in the village of Lundin Links, which derives its name from Lundin Links Golf Course, founded in 1868. This is a quiet little backwater and our home has commanding panoramic views over the wide estuary of the Firth of Forth.

The views are ever changing throughout the day with the interplay of light on the sea and sky. The view from our home across the water extends to Edinburgh, our capital, and is within easy reach of travel to the city. We enjoy the wonders of nature in this inspiring environment.

Largo is the adjoining village on the coast and this is descriptive of the pace of life in this beautiful unspoiled area of Scotland. It is aptly known as the East Neuk of Fife. The prevailing winds are from the South West and the East Neuk enjoys a micro climate as the clouds are parted by Largo Law, the hill behind the village.

We live 10 miles from St Andrews, where the Royal and Ancient Golf Club and course are known worldwide as the home of Golf. As we travel along the coast to St Andrews we pass through picturesque fishing villages of St. Monans, Anstruther and Pittenweem.

Moving a few miles inland we travel through rolling countryside known as the Howe of Fife. In other words this is a flat hollow of beautiful farmland. In Scottish history Falkland Palace was the seat of Kings, which accounts for the description 'The Kingdom of Fife'.

Largo Law

Lundin Links

Our home is in the village of Lundin Links overlooking the golf course.
Largo is the village on the coast beyond the golf course.

Largo Bay

Howe Of Fife

This is a photograph of the rolling countryside in the Howe of Fife

Howe Of Fife

The author completed all drawings and paintings in this book in the 1980's

Largo

Pittenweem Harbour

Old Course St Andrews

**Watercolour painting by
Scottish Artist John Mitchell R.S.W**
www.largoart.com

Princes Street Gardens

Magnificent views from the main street in Edinburgh

Home & Hearth

This is a drawing of our home and hearth

Home & Hearth

This is a photograph

Mantelpiece

The Mantelpiece is decorated with cards and ornaments

Lounge

We have a keen interest in art and collect paintings by Scottish artists, including Sir Robin Philipson, President of the RSA.

Candlestick

Candlelight

Foals Caprice

Sculpture by Phyllis Bone R.S.A.
Who was based in Edinburgh and was famed for animal sculptures

Soleil de Nuit

Sculpture by Erte

Conservatory

The painting in our conservatory is by our son Alastair who is a
master printmaker in Edinburgh Printmakers Workshop

Studio

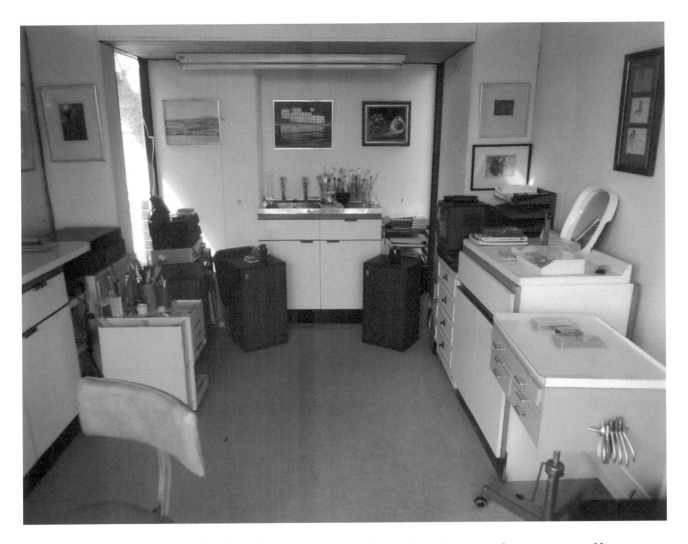

The art work in this book was completed at home in my studio

Home and Studio

All of the art work in this book was completed in my studio
at home in the 1980's as part of a correspondence course in art.

Sheila & Bill

Sheila is a wonderful companion
We have been married for 60 years

Sunrise

We have wonderful views from our home

Sunset

Sunset

Crimson ball, dressed in a scarlet gown
Gliding through the stratosphere.
Prima ballerina,
Tripping the light fantastic
Dancing and romancing with passing clouds.
Playing the perennial clown
In a circus of bright lights.

Merging into a yellow mist
Settling comfortably on the horizon,
A brilliant vision we dare not rest our eyes on.
Hovering to deliver
The last glimpse of daylight
Before disappearing into the night.

Everlasting enigma
What is your secret?
Do you party into the small hours,
Shedding light on a new hemisphere?
Where does your boundless energy come from?

We shiver when you disappear
Our whole world sleeps.
Every blade of grass, every flower
Birds, bees and butterflies
Every creature on God's earth
Depends on you for light and life.

Cosmic Queen of the universe
Surrounded by a galaxy of stars
In your presence their light pales into
insignificance
They bow to your every command
We cannot begin to understand
The full extent of your power.

Torran Lochan

Torran Lochan

For a moment the sun shone on the lochan and revealed to the full its rare and outstanding beauty.

This stemmed from the strong contrast presented by this little lochan to the majesty of the surrounding mountains.

The mountain peaks cleaved magnificently into the clouds as if they might disrupt the very sky with their grandeur.

The mountain slopes were rugged, sheer, desolate and unfriendly, cleft by cascading mountain streams and waterfalls, half hidden by white wisps of scurrying cloud.

Nestling comfortably at the foot of the mountains lay the lochan, fringed with fir trees and steeped in silence and intense stillness. The mountains cast a bold reflection on the still water.

Sheep grazed contentedly by the waterside and white gulls wheeled and skimmed gracefully to and fro' over the lochan.

Trout fretted the mirror surface of the water with circlets of ripples. All was peaceful and unspoiled. The lochan had a deep sense of timelessness.

There was here a wondrous equilibrium of life; that equilibrium which nature so easily acheives and man so often strives for.

Drawings

Drawings are the fundamental basis of art. Very often a quick sketch is the source of inspiration to create a work of art, by using the sketch to elaborate on the initial reaction to the subject and to go on to develop the theme to produce the final work.

This chapter illustrates sketches, begining with line drawings to develop coordination between hand and eye and to learn freedom of movement to produce lines and curves to develop skill in composition.

Progressing from line drawings we learn the rendering of light and shade or the use of colour to enhance the visual experience.

Choice of subject presents an endless variety of inspirational objects extending from the initial sketch through modelling to the graphic interpretation of form.

Then we proceed to more complex composition by assembling groups of objects to convey pleasing balance and symmetry, or equally imbalance and discord, depending on the subject and the interpretation we wish to convey.

This is a wholly absorbing and inspiring process to produce a work of art on a blank page using the simplest of tools to record and convey life and art as a visual experience for the artist and the viewer.

Scarecrow

Helter Skelter

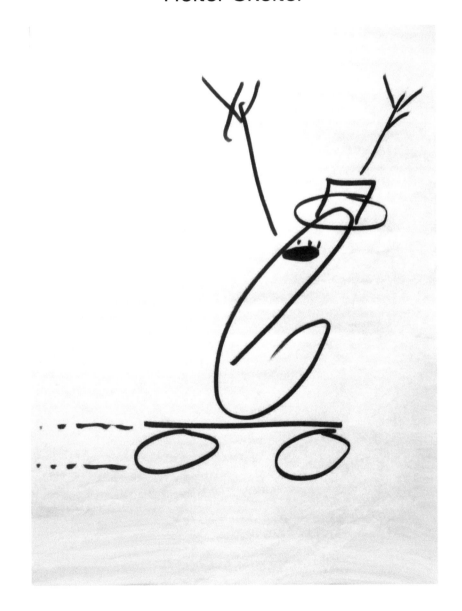

Poodle Doodle

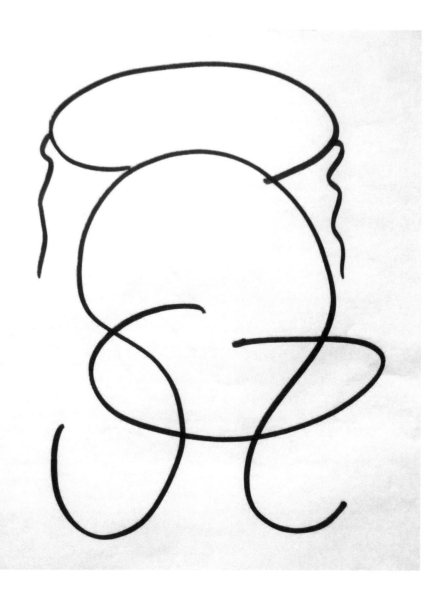

PanAm Shoe

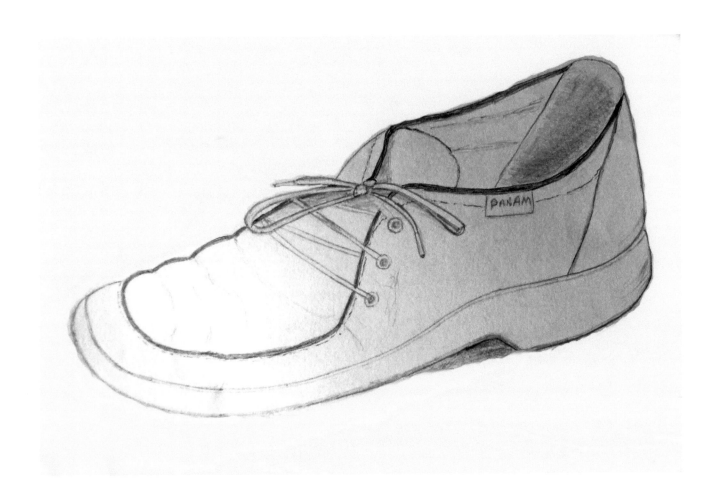

Hand

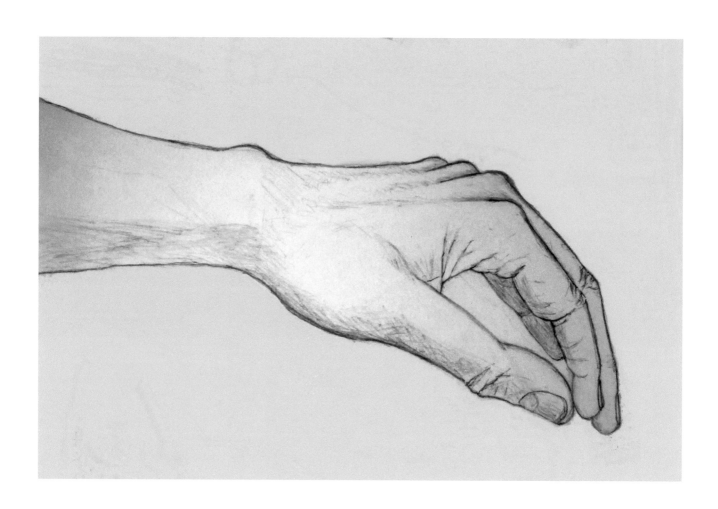

Foot

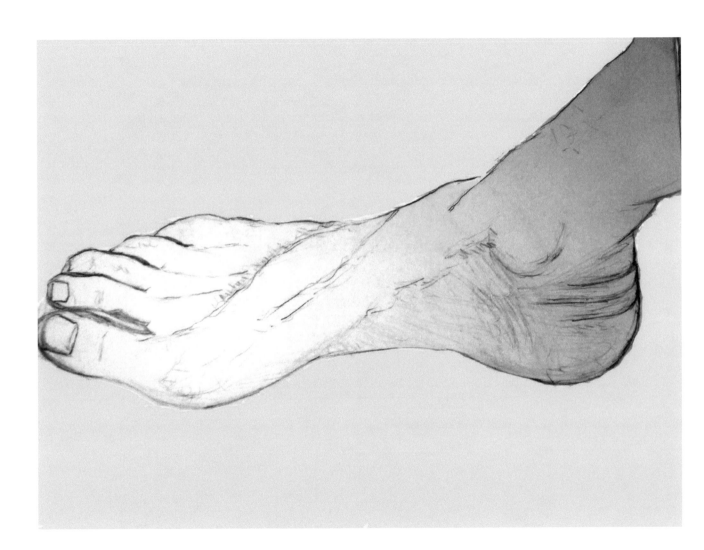

Sheila

Fiona

Candle Holder

Water Jug

Ormer Shell

Wine Bottle

Decanter

Wine Service

Reflections

Anchored

Dancing Twigs

Twiggy

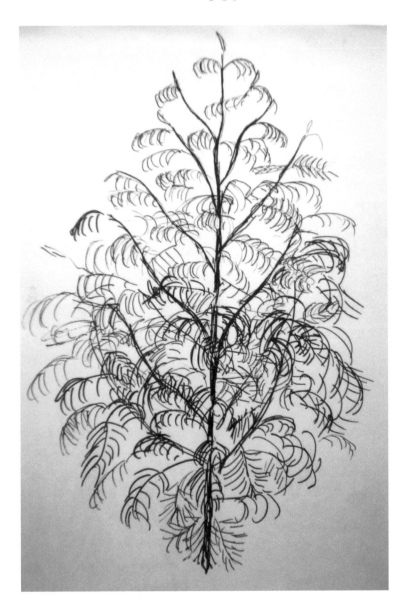

Rose Dance

Floral Dance

Drapery

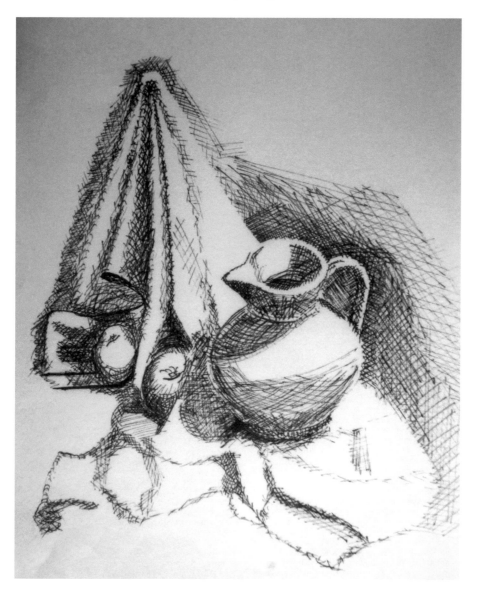

Lithograph

Moonlight

Moonlight

One of my earliest and most enduring memories from childhood is the Man in the Moon.

Little did I realize in those days that the benign face that smiled at me from billboards and packets of Creamola would play such a large part in our destiny.

There is no doubt that the man on the moon turned fiction dramatically into fact and heralded the dawn of the age of communication technology.

Since man became civilised, and even before that the moon has been a great source of inspiration in the arts, in music and literature.

I met the man in the moon again when we moved to our home overlooking the sea. I often have the feeling that he watches me as much as I watch him.

But when we describe moonlight we inevitably think of grace and elegance, changing moods, and the subtlety of the lady of the night. It is this indefinable quality of mystery which sets moonlight apart in our imagination.

Perhaps man is destined always to reach for the moon in a constant quest for the unattainable. Moonlight is an ideal, which defies description. That is part of its fatal attraction, and that is what tempted me to put into words some thoughts on moonlight.

Moonlight

Happy Creamola man
Laughing through a tracery of cloud,
To wink, and vanish in a halo of white mist
Master of mystery and disguise

Cosmic clown
Hiding under the cloak of night,
To burst forth with silvered kiss
Metamorphosis of an ethereal star

Lady of the night
Observing life through silver rimmed spectacles
Flirting with passionate wisps of cloud
Kissing indigo at midnight

Seductive circle
Caught in a dream of translucent thought
Weaving magical silhouettes
Spellbound

Opalescent pearl
Suspended at the throat of night
Revolving introspectively
To distil soft shadows into dark souls
In peaceful symbolism

Incandescent sphere
Rolling gently across the upturned bowl of night
Turning oceans
To spawn microbes and men
Who play at God
Fleetingly in an empty void

Cool iridescence
Turning an ever-changing face toward the earth
Exploding quietly
Upon the shuttered windows of consciousness
To touch a deeper chord of immortality

Transient mirage
Unseeing eyes chase mindless images across an empty sky
Seeking an illusion
Lucid candle dissolves counterfeit

Waxing and waning to a pale crescent
In quiet solitude

Silent messenger
Whispering secrets in a breath of wind
Speeding over continents, dismantling frontiers.
Spreading a meniscus of moonglow
Over the sheltering desert
The cool of night, a welcome relief
From the intense heat of day.

Jewel of night
Alight upon a sea of velvet
Stepping across oceans on tiptoe,
Casting luminescent shafts into the sea
To bounce like shattered crystal
Upon a distant shore
In a kaleidoscope of light.

Blythe spirit
Embracing mother earth
To enrich our souls in eternity

Circus Queen in centre stage
Surrounded by a galaxy of stars
Weaving a rich tapestry
Across the universe
Performing nocturnal pyrotechnics

Mystic vision
Floating past the sharp horizons of life
Reflecting life and love
Encased in a moving capsule of serenity and timelessness
Transcending immortality
To steal the thunder of a dying sun

White ghost
Etched in the open casements of a new day
Sliding through unnoticed

Cool fingered
Evocative moonlight
Ephemeral chameleon of the night

Still Life

The opening image in this chapter states that "Still Life is …A Bowl Of Cherries". That expresses the concept that in flowers, plants, vegetables, and fruit we have a world of eternal beauty and poetry always to hand.

However "Still Life" covers a wider concept of topics and subjects available to the artist to express beauty in form and balance and subtlety of light and shade.

Colour introduces a new dimension in the description and representation of form and structure in aesthetic terms. This chapter explores light and shade, colour and reflections using the concept of Still Life to describe and illustrate examples of this concept.

We may use any collection of inanimate objects to examine this principle. Creation of a composition relies on design and balance in order to create a collection of objects in a Still Life drawing or painting.

Composition in paint or pastel may deliver a pleasing image of assembled objects. This may include reflections or tints to represent the artists personal interpretation of Still Life.

Still Life is …. a Bowl of Cherries

Roses in a Copper Vase

Candlestick

Candlelight

Reflections

Liquid Lunch

Lobster

Fish Supper

Floral Study

Artist at Work

The Human Machine

Such are the wonders of modern science, that we have become blase about the miracle of life itself. Nowadays we do not bat an eyelid when we read in the newspapers or see on television reports on the imminent possibility of cloning human beings, or of sending space craft, manned or unmanned to some distant planet to carry out scientific research.

I remember two books which made an indelible impression on me when I was at school. They were George Orwell's '1984' and Aldous Huxley's 'Brave New World'. Both presented frightening visions of the future, which are uncomfortably close to the truth regarding aspects of Society today. Human cloning, for example, formed the basis for the regulated society depicted by Huxley in 'Brave New World' and Orwell's '1984' was uncomfortably close to strict state control in communist regimes.

Amid all this scientific wizardry, perhaps we have lost touch with the everyday miracles of life itself. Atomic research was making great strides in my schooldays. We learned that everything in the universe is made of incredibly tiny particles called atoms. If ten thousand million atoms were placed end to end, they would measure half an inch! Incredibly, an atom is like a solar system in miniature. The central sun, or nucleus has a number of planets or electrons orbiting around it. Different elements have different numbers of orbiting electrons.

Is it not amazing that any inanimate object we see is composed of atoms, integrated with bewildering complexity into a familiar form which remains recognisable and identifiable within our experience!

Atom is derived from the Greek *atomos,* meaning 'that which cannot be divided'. Typical of mankind's insatiable curiosity, we had no sooner discovered atoms, than we moved on to discover how to split the atom. The atomic bomb became an icon of our generation.

What is even more incomprehensible is the chemistry of life, otherwise known as biochemistry, whereby the 'holding of hands' by a chain of carbon-based molecules establishes a chain of life of incredible complexity.

Cloning is not new. Life begins as a single cell. It divides and at the same time multiplies, to produce a clone. At microscopic level this is the amoeboid experience.

Translate this, over aeons of development to the procreation of animals and humans by the same simplistic process of cellular division and multiplication, beginning from a single fertilised cell, we have evolved into an incredibly complex organism, the Human Machine.

Consider first that the blueprint for our familiar characteristics is contained on microscopic rod-shaped structures in the nucleus of a cell which is in the process of dividing. Thus, the DNA molecule in our chromosomes and genes is self-perpetuating and is responsible for passing hereditary characteristics from parents to offspring to determine many of our physical characteristics. Humankind evolves from a single cell with a built- in blueprint.

We are highly organised lumps of protoplasm with sophisticated systems for survival and procreation of our species.

First, we have an internal combustion engine which feeds on oxygen.
Every breath we take is a result of complex muscular synergy whereby we alternately expand and contract the rib cage to draw in air and expel carbon dioxide. This basic chemical interchange occurs in the lungs which resemble a pair of highly

vascular saclike respiratory organs. The activity of breathing normally occurs at subconscious level as involuntary muscle function is controlled in the posterior part of our brain, the cerebellum, which is equally well developed throughout the animal kingdom.

Food is our fuel. It is propelled through the mouth into a long tube, passing quickly into the abdomen, where it enters a convoluted muscular tube. Food is broken down first in the mouth and then in the intestine where the most useful constituents are absorbed. Indigestible components of food, such as fibre continue to pass through the large intestine before being excreted in what must be one of the less dignified aspects of human behaviour.

The liver is similar to a storage and processing plant for food, prior to its distribution through the bloodstream to repair and regenerate tissues throughout the body, and also to provide the energy we require to complete our bodily functions.

Next we have an internal transport system which puts British Rail to shame. Oxygen is conveyed in disc shaped red corpuscles floating in the blood plasma. Red corpuscles are so small that a pin head contains 5 million of them. Oxygenated blood passes from the lungs to the heart, the central pumping station, with its four chambers working in harmony to propel the blood throughout the body. Blood distribution via the arteries ends in a delicate network of capillaries to deposit nutrients to the innumerable cells which make up the tissues throughout the body, before returning to the lungs to expel carbon dioxide.

In addition to the life-giving processes of food and oxygen distribution, blood circulation also removes waste products from the tissues and fights disease and infection through the white blood corpuscles. Blood performs another important function by distributing heat evenly as it remains at a constant temperature.

The human sewage system uses the kidneys as filters for waste products. It shares the urinary tract with the sexual and reproductive system. Our method of procreation is similar to other mammals and we have made little progress in refining this aspect of human behaviour.

The most fascinating component of the human machine is our computer system. The shoulder-top version puts the desk-top, lap-top and palm-top computers in the shade! It is the nerve centre of an amazing electro-chemical control system. It computes information from all five sensory receptors and simultaneously distributes instructions via the spinal column and peripheral nervous system to control our physical, intellectual and social interaction with our environment. This is information technology at its most sophisticated. The human brain is equivalent to the entire telecommunications system throughout the world.

Physical control alone is absolutely mind boggling! Our body is supported by a muscular and skeletal framework. Each fibre of each muscle has a nerve ending which is connected to the brain. Messages pass to and from the brain to control simultaneously each movement of every muscle in the body. Even the simplest movement requires delicate control of muscles with opposing actions to act in balance. Lifting a forkful of food to the mouth is a miracle of engineering skill. If the nerve pathways are interrupted by disease or disability, observe the incredible effort required to perform the simplest tasks.

The Senses

Sight, hearing, smell, taste and touch,
The senses propel us
Through the fascinating journey of life.
The eye, an orbit of sight interprets light
In all its glorious splendour.

The tongue, that intelligent muscle
Plays with the lips to form
Fricatives and sibilants,
Each in our own language
Of accent and dialect
To communicate with our peers

The ears our receptors of sound
From spoken voice to symphony orchestra
Taste and smell are related brothers
Our twin olfactory organs

Touch is universal
From fingertips to tongue and lips
Exploring the horizons of life
In a myriad of spectacular sensations

The Human Machine is indeed a miraculous organism.

Now we come to the crunch!
If we have such a wonderful Human Machine
Is it truly perfect, or are there fatal flaws
In the make-up of humankind?

We delude ourselves into believing that we are the ultimate,
Or even the most important step in the evolutionary chain.
Not so, my friends, we are not perfect.
We are simply one step on the ladder of evolution.
We shall become extinct as surely as the dinosaurs before us.
Especially if we continue to abuse our atmosphere and environment
Planet earth may die sooner than we think.

On The Beach

This chapter is based on a beach holiday in the Greek island of Skiathos in the 1980's. While enjoying sunshine in a holiday mode this was an opportunity to record activities on the beach and to interpret these experiences with artistic liscence.

Holidays are an important part of our lives as we escape from the daily routine into a peaceful environment with time to unwind. This provides an ideal scenario to observe typical images as we relax and enjoy a holiday on the beach.

It was fascinating to watch and record behaviour as we interact with recreational activities expressing our individual response to the freedom from the confines of everyday life. We are released from work to play and express our individual personality in a quiet environment of rest and relaxation.

This brings images into sharp relief from a paddling seagul to sailing, diving, sleeping, relaxing, reading and beachcombing.

Meantime we have the opportunity to interpret sights and sounds of multiple activities, typical of a sun seeking holiday. We may be on top of the world or otherwise occupied as we relax on the beach.

Paddling

Anchor Away

Diver

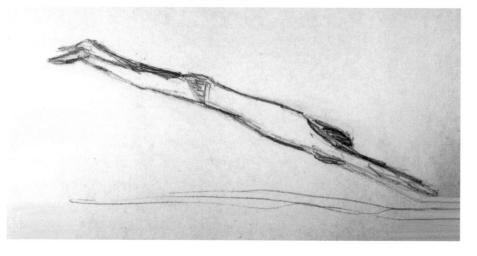

Sailing

Berthed

Sleeping Figures

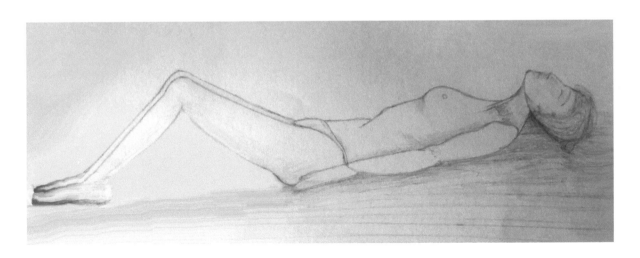

Relaxing

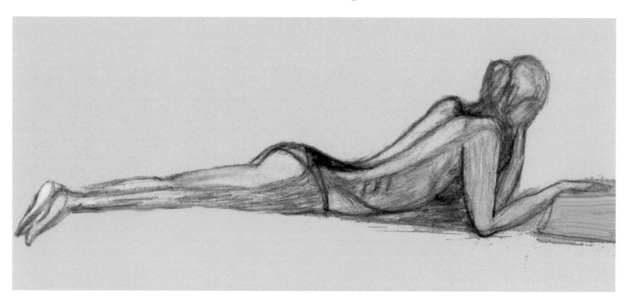

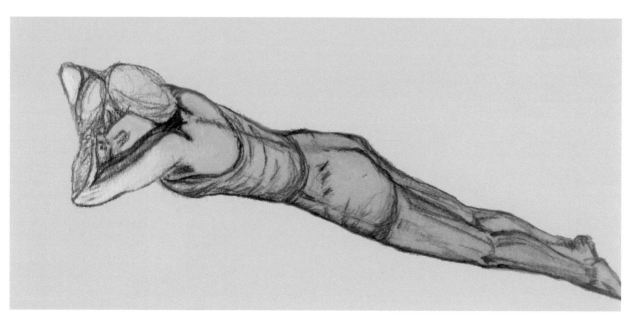

Resting

Reading

Pipe Smoking

Beachcombing

Digging

On Top Of The World

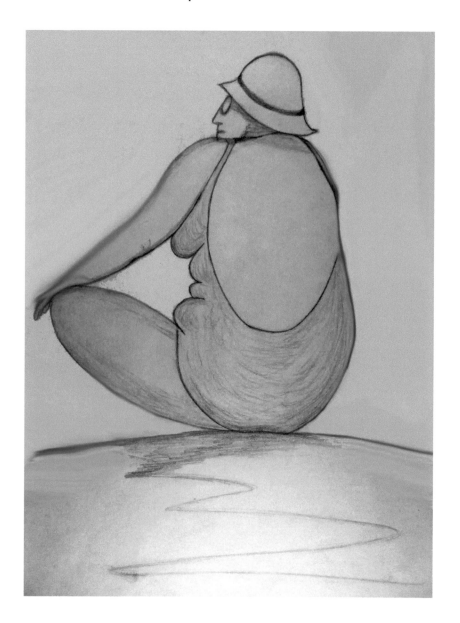

Sunglasses

Rear View

Feet Up

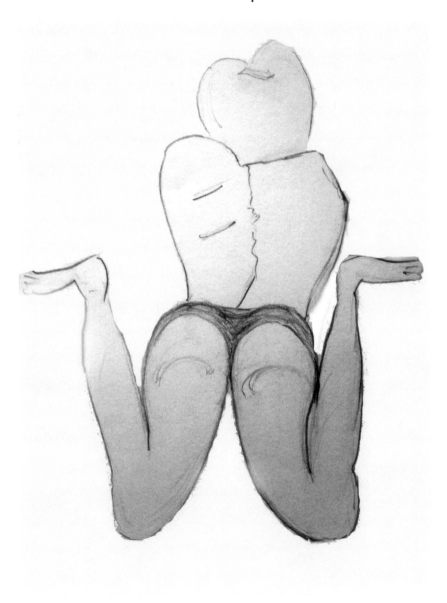

Sailor

Anchored

Outboard Motor Man

Asleep

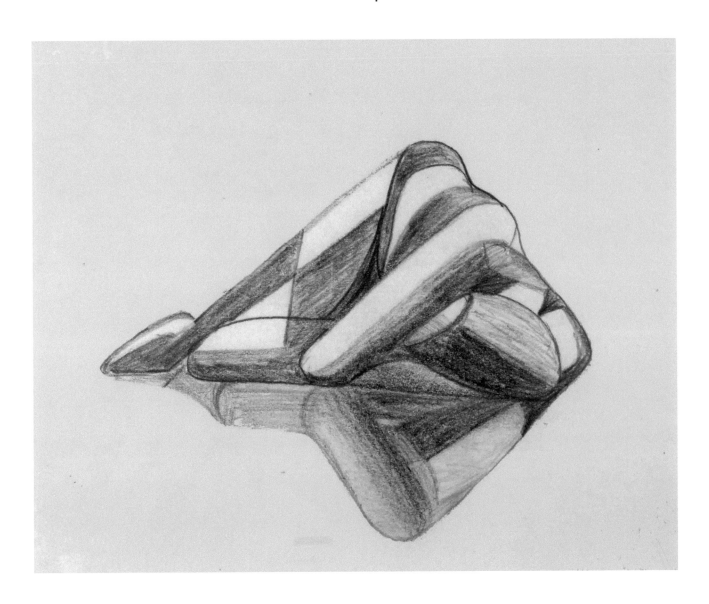

Dead Cow Dancing

The Whisky Trail

The Whisky trail is a tourist attraction
Fraught with danger
For many a stranger
To our native shores

You can rest assured
That a sightseeing tour
Of Highland distilleries
Or new fangled wineries
Will lead to disaster
And you being plastered
If you brave the Scotch mist
You'll get quietly pissed

Hogmanay is a Scottish invention
To undermine aspects of boring convention
It loosens our tongue
And helps us have fun
Mum gets quite merry
On one glass of sherry
While your maiden aunt is able to chant
As she scoffs all your brandy
"It's always quite handy
For medicinal purposes of course!"

This problem is not
Confined to the Scots
An American requires
To maintain his sobriety
And proper propriety
While knocking back endless martinis

An innocent jaunt to South California
Is inclined to initiate senile dementia
Quite prematurely, of course
If we visit their wineries
And sample their fineries
Before we come staggering home

"Just drop in for cocktails"
Is sure to entail
An early resumption
Of excessive consumption
Of weird combinations
And deadly concoctions
Like bourbon and Scotch
With gin on the rocks
When I am already
A trifle unsteady

Even the Germans
Are equally determined
That a cruise down the Rhine
Is knee deep in wine
Not to mention the fear
Of their very strong beer

From comrades and Ruskies
To Eskimos and Huskies
From the Nile to the Volga
And from Schnapps
To neat Vodka

We fuddle and muddle and guddle our way
Through life on the Whisky Trail

Just One For The Road

Before you have that other drink,
Pause for a moment, please, and think.
Is it reasonable to assume,
Taking into account the revolving room,
That if your last glass of whisky
Left you feeling pleasantly frisky
It does not necessarily follow
That if you have another swallow
That oozy feeling in your brain
Will disappear and leave no pain

I must admit that a glass of wine
Sipped and tasted as you dine
Is undeniably very fine
And there is no question
That it aids your digestion
In due moderation, of course

I cannot stress to you too much
That your constitution is such
That when you imbibe
If you oversubscribe
It will rot all your liver
And then make you shiver,
A dithering, blithering idiot
Whisky will lead you on the road to ruin
Because of the state that it will get you in!

I do believe you're turning pale
And taking note of this cautionary tale
Unless of course you're feeling sick
Punctuated with a loud ...... "HIC"

Moderation is the keyword
If you feel you list to leeward
You should pause and contemplate
What other dangers lie in wait
You are likely to regurgitate
If you dare to tempt your fate
With "JUST ONE FOR THE ROAD"

Flower Drawings

This chapter is based on a series of assignments on plants and flowers. In flowers, plants and vegetables we have a world of eternal beauty and poetry always to hand.

Flower drawings are popular subjects in training the hand and eye to represent images from nature. This is an important aspect in the process of adopting a personal style for any prospective student of art. Flower drawings are well represented at all levels of teaching and in art literature.

We have easy access to a wide range of beautiful designs that present a challenge to produce images worthy of Floral Art.

Flowers can be studied either in sumptuous floral arrangements or outdoors in their natural state. They are the perfect vehicle for artistic expression. Their bold sinuous curves, their grace and elegance always inspire a feeling of balance and harmony. Line drawings represent an ideal medium for the artist to develop a personal perspective and style in learning the elements of artistic expression.

The intricate design of leaves is equally challenging for the artist to convey the structure of plants. Variegated patterns offer an additional challenge to convey in a flower drawing.

Roses

Rose Twig

Single Rose

Rose & Leaf

Rose Silhouette

Coleus Leaves

Coleus Sprig

Coleus Plant

Coleus Cutting

Angel Trumpets

Flower Jug

Little Brown Jug

Floral Dance

Humankind

I am a speck of dust
Floating in the vastness of space
Unimportant
Invisible
Insignificant
Smaller than a grain of sand

In the context of
Eternity and immortality.
My ideas are important
Only to me!
I am not
Powerful or influential
I am merely a human being

I am a speck of dust
Upon a speck of dust
That is the earth
Revolving in the universe,
A mere flicker
Upon the consciousness of humankind

Life is but a short sequence of thoughts
And sensations
Waking and sleeping
And wakening again
Travelling briefly down the corridor of time
That we call Life.

Humankind is a myriad of dust
Scattered across the sands of time.

Locomotion

Miraculous mandarin
Adenosine tri-phosphatase,
Building block of life
Architect of movement
Cycling through narrow lanes
To halt in a capillary bed
At some appointed junction
Feeding some distant muscle
Through its malolactic phase

Each synaptic response
Represents a single aspect of communication
To control each muscle fibre
In a complex engine
Of interdependent pistons and levers
Timed to a millisecond
Tuned to perfection
To achieve synergy
In the constant ebb and flow
Of waking and sleeping,
Walking and breathing
Without thinking!

Each breath we take,
Every blink of an eye,
A miracle of locomotion
The sheer wonder of animation
In the equilibrium of life

Seduction

Morning greeting
To a solitary rose.
Velvet petals, dew dipped in tears,
A shivering cocoon
Trapped in a net of white gossamer
Imprisoned
In the prickly forest of an alien host
Quivering in solitude

Open your heart
To the warmth of the morning sun
Release your mystic potions
And seduce the deadly thorns,
Your devoted guardians
Of beauty and splendour.
Softly kiss uncaring joy
Into the heart of my loved one
This quiet morning.

Floral Art

This chapter expresses the wonder of nature in perpetuating the exquisite form of Floral Art.

Placing this in perspective, representing floral images is one of the finest challenges of interpretaion throughout centuries of artistic development.

Floral Art is the ulimate expression of beauty in the natural world. The combination of colour and form makes floral paintings one of the most emotive subjects of still life and aesthetic art.

On a personal level I have enjoyed this aspect of artistic expression as a means of interpreting the wonders of nature.

The world of nature cannot be replicated by humankind. Irrespective of our technical skills in imagery and digital technology we could not make a flower. Yet we can observe the incredible variety of Floral Art produced by nature in a fascinating sequence of design and colour.

We are priviledged to observe the sheer beauty and inventiveness of the natural world.

Floral Art

Flowers in a Gilded Vase

Bouquet in a Lustre Jug

Roses in a Copper Vase

Flowers in a Glass Vase

Dancing Flowers

Ballet Dancers

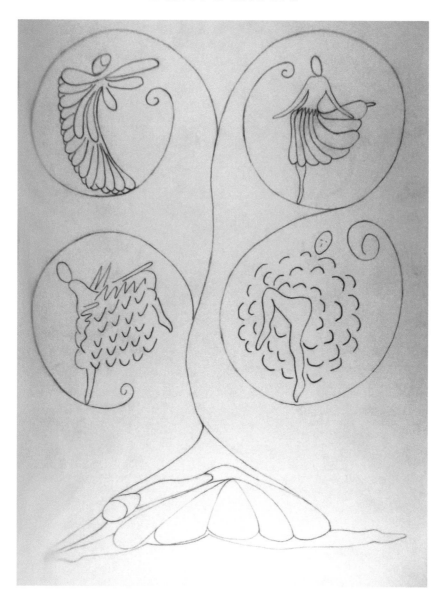

Corps De Ballet

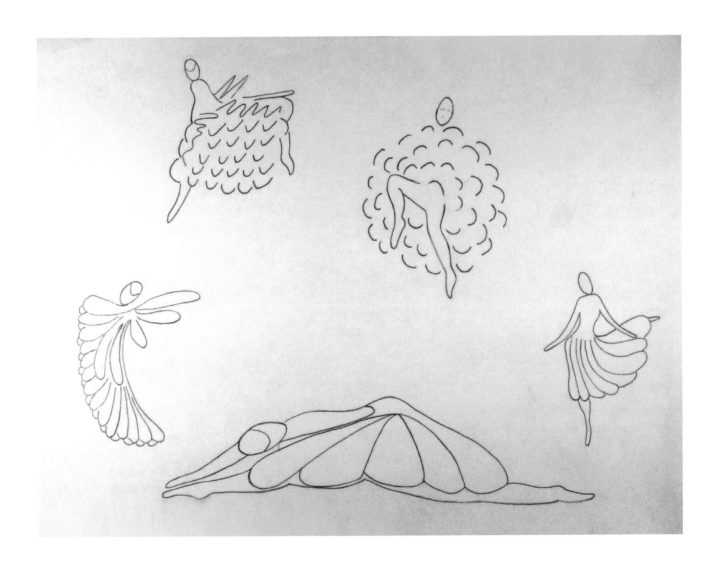

Rehearsal

Prima Ballerima

Moonshine

Moonshine

Urgent black clouds flit across the sky
The moon peeps discreetly round them
Etching their edges in silver incandescent light
Like smooth white silk.

It is raining – pleasant soft unhurried rain
Swirling in the gentle breeze,
Dancing in puddles
Whispering on my forehead.

The moon escapes from its confinement
First its full yellow rim
Then its plump kindly face
Smiling at the winking stars.

The surrounding sky
Brilliant seared apricot
Merges imperceptibly
To a cool enamelled greyness

As the sky grows scarlet in the east
The Moon settles comfortably on the horizon
Like a contented old man
Sinking into his armchair

Moonshine

Cat Naps

When our family were young we had pets. They added another dimension to family life at home.

It is no accident that a dog is described as man's best friend. For many years our black labrador, Cleo was the most faithful and devoted of pets, expressing mutual love and affection to the entire family.

Later we added cats to our family and contrary to common belief Cleo was equally tolerant of the cats and would happily sleep with them. These were no ordinary cats because they were Siamese, the aristocats of the cat family!

Cleo adopted Ming as a surrogate friend. Ming had little imperfections that are a frequent trait in some Siamese cats. He had a squint and a kink in his tail, but he and Cleo were close friends and companions.

Ming's brother, Chang was a true Aristocat. Chang had a regal presence and carried himself with great pride and confidence.

Leisha, an anagram of Sheila was a Siamese Foreign Black. She had grace and elegance in abundance.

Siamese Cats have a good life, with plenty of time for Cat Naps. That makes them an ideal subject for still life studies, interspersed by periods of activity.

China Cat

Sleepy Cat

Leisha

Cat Nap

Chang

Ming

Cleo Sleeping

Sleepy Cats

Cat Alert

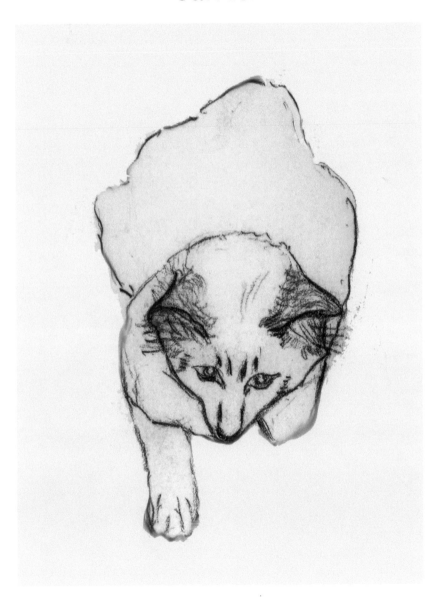

Cat Naps

On Guard

Fluff

Fluffy

Snooze

Slumbering Cats

Paws For Thought

Dozing

To an Ant   On seeing him flooded from his home, 2013

Wee, proud an' han'some soldier
Clad in medieval suit of armour
Thou need not rin awa sae hasty
        Frae my attention
I wad be laith to rin an' chase thee
        To thy detention

I'm truly sorry God's dominion
Has broken nature's social union
By invading your proud kingdom
        Wi' tempestuous seas
An' occupying man's dominion
        With consumate ease!

I doubt na, whyles, but thou may thieve;
What then? Poor beastie, thou maun live!
A peck o' dirt upon the floor
        'S a sma' request
An' leavin' quietly through the door
        Back to your nest

Thou saw the towns laid bare an'waste
Wi' rivers runnin' down the streets;
An' cozie down, beneath the blast,
        Thou chose to dwell.
Till crash! The cruel water passed
        To flood thy nest!

Thy wee bit housie's now in ruin!
The heavy rain its floors a'floodin'
An' can't afford to build a new yin
        On village green
Wi' Januar's snow an' wind ensuin'
          Baith snell an' keen

Thy wee bit heap o' dung an' rubble
Has cost thee many a weary hobble
Now thou's undone, for a' thy trouble
        Out of house and hame
To thole the winter's sleety dribble
        An' freezin' cauld

But, Antie, thou art not thy lane,
In proving foresight is in vain:
The best laid schemes of mice and men
        Gang aft agley
An' leave us nought but grief an' pain
        An' broken promises

But thou art blest, compared wi' me:
The present only toucheth thee
While I look back in memory,
        To times that went before.
You enjoy your reverie
        As you run across the floor

The Humble Ant

I want you to imagine that you are an ant
Living in a commune underground
The quintessential feudal state
You are either a worker or a soldier,
Unless you happen to be a queen!

Your appearance is not exactly endearing,
But you are an incredible miracle
Of biological engineering.
Sensitive antennae,
Six hairy legs and fearsome jaws:
You punch above your weight
With your sharp claws!

Collectively you are way ahead of man!
Your community sticks to an organised plan
To serve your queen in harmony,
Sacrificing life and limb to protect her royalty.
The ultimate example of devoted loyalty.

Despite your size
You win a prize
You are a formidable adversary!

Holiday Art

Holidays offer an ideal opportunity of spare time to catch up on leisure activities.

This chapter is based on holidays in the Algarve and Corfu when I was sketching and painting.

Once again sketches are based on the surrounding scenes to capture the features of the landscapes. Lake views are always inspiring picturesque subjects, while trees offer striking silhouettes.

Ripples and reflections on the sea are captured first by photographs as a basis for intepretation in a painting.

A relaxing holiday in the sun gives the opportunity to draw and paint surrounding scenery and my hand and foot offer a challenge to produce a tinted drawing.

The Corfu Planter at our villa provides another opportunity to have fun in the sun. That is the basis for Holiday Art.

Villa

Algarve Terrace

Quinta do Lago

Lake View

Trees & Lake

Fir Trees

Tree Silhouettes

Sailing Ship

Seascape

Ripples & Reflections

Ripples & Reflections

Hand

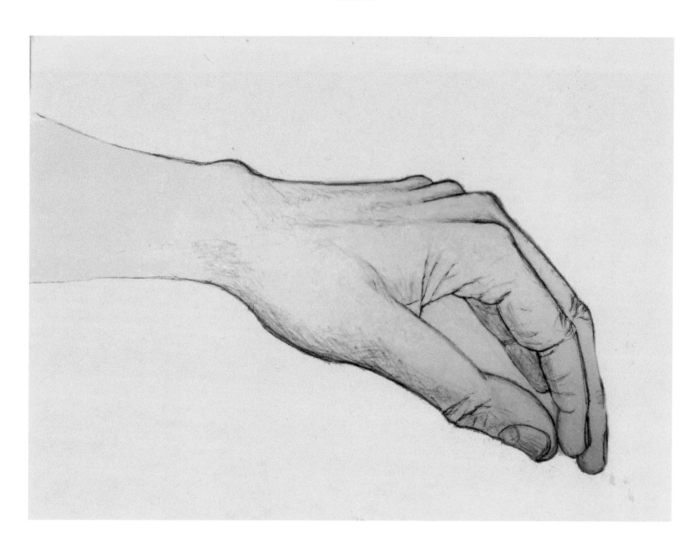

Foot

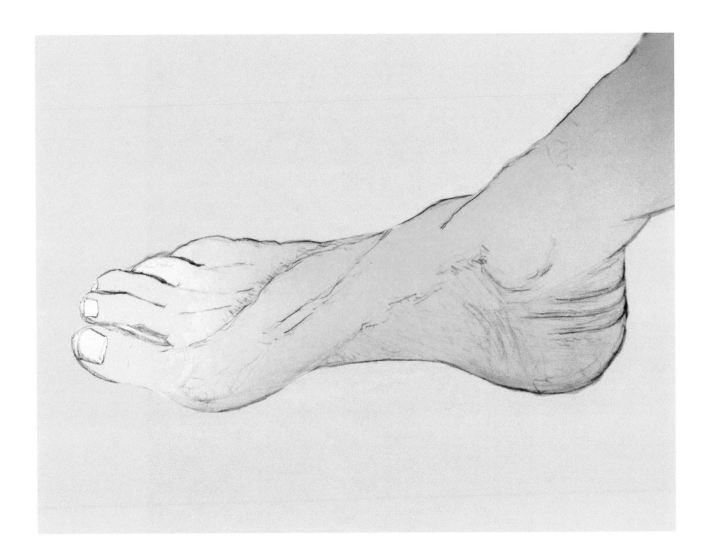

Planter

Beach Boy

Alastair

Fiona's Art

Type to enter text

Now we have a little light relief to finish on a personal note!

Bill's Trills

When I was young
I would have loved to play the piano
We didn't have a piano
So that put paid to that ambition.
Before Television we listened to music
I was inspired by Benny Goodman
The combination of jazz and classical music
Convinced me that I might follow in his footsteps
Having never shown any musical talent at school.

My mother and father showed great faith in me
When they bought a second-hand clarinet,
I couldn't read music,
Never mind play the instrument
But my school motto was PERSEVERANDO
I continued to produce an endless series
Of shrill squeaks, screeches and wrong notes
With this unsuspecting clarinet.
The beauty of music is that
You don't have to play it to enjoy it.
In fact sometimes it is better if you don't play it!

My parents are living to regret their investment
In my musical career!
At this stage I never did master the clarinet
Eventually it was put away in its case.
When I went to University to study dentistry.

Fast forward to the 1990's
Now our family have flown the nest,
In my sixties I settle down to tackle music seriously!
I added a saxophone to my repertoire
I finally learn to read music
I begin to enjoy this new experience
Of playing an instrument.
This could be the start of my musical career!

At home there is a room we fondly call
my 'music room' where I practice solo.
Speaking from personal experience
I have Bruised Brahms,
Beaten Beethoven,
Murdered Mozart,
Shocked Schubert
Tortured Tchaikovsky,
And that is only the classical repertoire!

Bill's Trills

That brings us to the other element of music.
Jazz has its roots
In the gospel songs of African Americans
In the deep south, it is characterized by
The Blue Note, a fusion of
African and European musical traditions
With improvisation and syncopation.
I never mastered them either!

But now I can happily
Grind out Gershwin,
Punish Charlie Parker,
Shoot Scott Joplin
Kill Aker Bilk
And they are all turning in their graves!

Muskat Ramble,
Yardbird Suite,
Harlem Nocturne,
You name it I can assault it
To inflict grievous bodily harm
On your ear drums.

One of my favourite numbers is Desafinado,
Which, literally translated means
'Slightly out of tune'.
How appropriate!

But when I close the door of my music room
I am transported into the
Magical, Mystical World of Music.

That is when I play Bill's Trills

I hope you have enjoyed this trip down memory lane
My heartfelt thanks to Sheila for her help in editing
I coudn't do it without her support
We recently celebrated 60 years together with our
diamond wedding

Dr William Clark
Orthodontics Pioneer

For those of you not familiar with the term, orthodontics is a specialized area of dentistry concerned with the realignment of improperly aligned teeth. Dr William Clark specialized in orthodontics in the early 1960's after qualifying as a dentist and has practiced orthodontics for 50 years. Creativity, hard work, dedication and his development of innovative techniques in orthodontics and dentofacial orthopaedics have led to him becoming a leading figure in his field.

In 1977 he invented Twin Blocks, a new functional technique to advance the mandible in treatment of patients with a weak or receding chin. In addition to improving facial appearance this has holistic benefits, by moving the tongue forward and increasing the airway. This concept can also be used in treatment of patients with sleep apnoea, who have difficulty breathing at night and suffer from tiredness during the day.

In 1990 he presented the first teleconference in clinical dentistry in a live course in Chicago, transmitted by satellite to 25 cities in the USA and Canada. This launched his techniques and for the past 30 years he has travelled worldwide to deliver courses and lectures in over 55 countries. His informal presentation of complex material, combined with detailed illustrations and case reports, helps him to convey knowledge to participants on courses at different levels of experience. He has used this same approach in his 3 recently completed ebooks, 'Faces & Braces', 'Advances in Fixed Appliance Technique' and 'Advances in Functional Therapy & Dentofacial Orthopaedics'.

'Faces & Braces' illustrates the benefits of orthodontic treatment for patients and parents, showing how treatment can improve their appearance and give them a confident smile.

'Advances in Fixed Appliance Technique' and 'Advances in Functional Therapy & Dentofacial Orthopaedics' are designed to educate professionals and staff in dental and orthodontic practice.

Dr Clark has been happily married for 60 years and although he would like to have more time to spend with his wife and family and to develop his other interests, such as playing the saxophone and clarinet, he is not ready to retire quite yet. He plans to continue to travel and give courses for as long as he is fit and able.

Please visit Twinblocks for more information on e-books, courses and techniques.

Lightning Source UK Ltd.
Milton Keynes UK
UKHW050414290920
370700UK00002B/70

9 781728 355269